Encounters with God

The Gospel of JOHN

Encounters with God

The Gospel of JOHN

Published by Thomas Nelson, Inc., P.O. Box 141000, Nashville, Tennessee 37214.

Scripture quotations are taken from The New King James Version® (NKJV), copyright 1979, 1980, 1982, 1992 Thomas Nelson, Inc., Publishers.

Library of Congress Cataloging-in-Publication Data
ISBN 1-4185-2641X 9781418526412

Printed in the United States of America

07 08 09 10 RRD 9 8 7 6 5 4 3 2 1

CONTENTS

AN INTRODUCTION TO THE GOSPEL OF JOHN

The Gospel of John is the fourth book of the New Testament. As a Gospel, it truly presents the good news of Jesus—what Jesus did, what He said, and who He was. This Gospel differs, however, from the synoptic Gospel accounts of Matthew, Mark, and Luke in several significant ways.

First, the Gospel of John is more theological—it focuses on the divine nature of Jesus. The miracles of Jesus are not regarded as demonstrations of power as much as they are signs that point to Jesus' heavenly origin and authority. John's purpose was to present Jesus in a way that convinced readers of His deity.

Second, John did not include many of the events or details found in the other three Gospel accounts. Many people believe John was writing twenty or more years after the other Gospels were written and that he likely had access to one or more of them. He may have been writing to *fill in the gaps* or, in a few cases, to add greater detail. His audience was not limited to either Jews or Gentiles—John was writing to all believers with a distinct purpose rooted not only in his eyewitness experience of Jesus' life and ministry, but also his first-hand experience in how the church lived out the life and ministry of Jesus for more than half a century.

Third, John dealt in a special way with the words *love, word, light, and believe*—especially as these concepts are related to the nature and ministry of Jesus. The book presents the contrasts all Christians face: light and darkness, belief and unbelief, and life and death. The Gospel of John emphasizes the love *of* God manifested by Christ Jesus, and our love *for* God manifested most vividly by our obedience to Christ's commandments. Jesus taught that believers' love for one another would convince the world that Christians are Jesus' disciples (see John 17:21). John appears to voice a hearty Amen!

John's Gospel is a thematic presentation of Jesus' life, not a chronological account. John focuses on seven of Jesus' *I am* statements that describe His identity: *the bread of life* (6:35,41,48,51); *the light of the world* (8:12; 9:5); *the door of the sheep* (10:7,9); *the good shepherd* (10:11,14); *the resurrection and the life* (11:25); *the way, the truth, and the life* (14:6); and *the true vine* (15:1,5). The Jews, of course, had a strong concept of God the Father as *I am*—He was and is and will be without changing, both eternal and in the moment, always the omnipotent and omniscient God. The *I am* statements of Jesus are a definitive claim of His deity as God the Son.

John also focused on seven specific signs that clearly revealed Jesus' divinity: changing water to wine (2:1–11), healing a man's son (4:46–54), healing a lame man (5:1–9), feeding five thousand men (6:1–14), walking on water (6:15–21), healing a blind man (9:1–7), and raising Lazarus from the dead (11:38–44).

To the Jews, the number *seven* was associated with perfection and completion. John presented Jesus as the perfection and completion of God's nature and power.

Throughout the centuries, the Gospel of John has been one of the most popular Bible books in Christianity. Perhaps no Scripture has been more memorized or been more instrumental in conversions to Christ than John 3:16. That was John's intent! He said of his own Gospel account he was writing "that you may believe that Jesus is the Christ, the Son of God, and that believing you may have life in His name" (John 20:31).

John the Author. Although John never identifies himself as the apostle John, brother of James, or as one of the sons of Zebedee, he has been considered to be all of the above since the earliest days of Christianity. Rather than laying claim to being part of Jesus' inner circle, the author of the Gospel refers to himself as "the disciple whom Jesus loved" (13:23; 19:26; 20:2; 21:7, 20). This phrase is not meant to imply an exclusive relationship, but rather, it is an expression of the great love that John felt from Jesus, both during Jesus' lifetime and by the power of Holy Spirit through the years after Jesus' ascension to heaven. John lived and wrote from the perspective of one who knew Jesus well, and had experienced the depth of Christ's love and forgiveness.

Tradition holds John took the gospel message to Asia Minor, which we know primarily as Turkey today. He was instrumental in establishing seven major churches there and became the bishop over those churches, with his headquarters in Ephesus. He was imprisoned for a period of several years on the island of Patmos, where he wrote the book of Revelation. The letters of 1 John, 2 John, and 3 John likely were written prior to both the Gospel of John and Revelation.

AN OVERVIEW OF OUR STUDY
OF THE GOSPEL OF JOHN

This study guide presents seven lessons drawn from and based largely on the Gospel of John. The study guide elaborates on, and is based on, the commentary included in the *Blackaby Study Bible*:

Lesson #1: Jesus Is God's Word

Lesson #2: Jesus Is the True Light

Lesson #3: Jesus Is the Bread of Life from Heaven

Lesson #4: Jesus Is the Good Shepherd

Lesson #5: Jesus Is the Life–Giver

Lesson #6: Jesus Is the Vine

Lesson #7: Jesus Is the Sacrificial Lamb for the Forgiveness of Sin

Personal or Group Use. These lessons are offered for personal study and reflection, or for small-group Bible study. The questions may be answered by an individual reader, or used as a foundation for group discussion. A segment titled "Notes to Leaders of Small Groups" is included at the back of this book to help those who might lead a group study of the material.

Before you embark on this study, we encourage you to read in full "How to Study the Bible" in the *Blackaby Study Bible* on pages viii–ix. The Bible is unique among all literature. It is God's definitive word for humanity. The Bible is

- *inspired*—God breathed

- *authoritative*—absolutely the final word on any spiritual matter

- *the plumb line of truth*—the standard against which all human activity and reasoning must be evaluated

The Bible is fascinating in that it has remarkable diversity, but also remarkable unity. The books were penned by a diverse assortment of authors representing a variety of languages and cultures. The Bible as a whole has a number of literary forms. But, the Bible's message from cover to cover is clear, consistent, and unified.

More than mere words on a page, the Bible is an encounter with God Himself. No book is more critical to your life. The very essence of the Bible is the Lord Himself.

God speaks by the Holy Spirit through the Bible. He also communicates during your time of prayer, in your life circumstances, and through the church. Read your Bible in an attitude of prayer, and allow the Holy Spirit to make you aware of God's activity in and through your personal life. Write down what you learn, meditate on it, and adjust your thoughts, attitudes, and behavior accordingly. Look for ways every day in which the truth of God's Word can be applied to your circumstances and relationships. God is not random, but orderly and intentional in the way He speaks to you.

Be encouraged—the Bible is *not* too difficult for the average person to understand if that person asks the Holy Spirit for help. (Furthermore, not even the most brilliant person can fully understand the Bible apart from the Holy Spirit's help!) God desires for you to know Him and His Word. Every person who reads the Bible can learn from it. The one who will receive maximum benefit from reading and studying the Bible, however, is the person who:

- *is born again* (John 3:3, 5). Those who are born again and have received the gift of God's Spirit have a distinct advantage in understanding the deeper truths of His Word.

- *has a heart that desires to learn God's truth*. Your attitude greatly influences the outcome of Bible study. Resist the temptation to focus on what others have said about the Bible. Allow the Holy Spirit to guide you as you study God's Word for yourself.

- *has a heart that seeks to obey God*. The Holy Spirit teaches most of those who have a desire to apply what they learn. Begin your Bible study with prayer, asking the Holy Spirit to guide your thoughts and to impress upon you what is on God's heart. Then, make plans to adjust your life immediately to obey the Lord fully.

As you read and study the Bible, your purpose is not to *create* meaning, but to *discover* the meaning of the text with the Holy Spirit's guidance. Ask yourself, "What did the author have in mind? How was this applied by those who first heard these words?" Especially in your study of the Gospel accounts, pay attention to the words of Jesus that begin "Most assuredly" or "He opened His mouth and taught them, saying." These are core principles and teachings that powerfully impact every person's life.

At times you may find it helpful to consult other passages of the Bible (made available in the center columns in the *Blackaby Study Bible*), or the commentary in the margins of the Blackaby Study Bible.

Keep in mind always that Bible study is not primarily an exercise for acquiring information, but an opportunity for transformation. Bible study is your opportunity to encounter God and to be changed in His presence. When God speaks to your heart, nothing remains the same. Jesus said, "He who has ears to hear, let him hear" (Matthew 13:9). Choose to have ears that desire to hear!

The B-A-S-I-Cs of Each Study in This Guide. Each lesson in this study guide has five segments, using the word BASIC as an acronym. The word BASIC does not allude to elementary or simple, but rather to *foundational*. These studies extend the concepts that are part of the *Blackaby Study Bible* commentary and are focused on key aspects of what it means to be a Christ-follower in today's world. The BASIC acronym stands for:

B = *Bible Focus.* This segment presents the central passage for the lesson and a general explanation that covers the central theme or concern.

A = *Application for Today.* This segment has a story or illustration related to modern-day times, with questions that link the Bible text to today's issues, problems, and concerns.

S = *Supplementary Scriptures to Consider.* In this segment, other Bible verses related to the general theme of the lesson are explored.

I = *Introspection and Implications.* In this segment, questions are asked that lead to deeper reflection about one's personal faith journey and life experiences.

C = *Communicating the Good News.* This segment presents challenging questions aimed at ways in which the truth of the lesson might be lived out and shared with others (either to win the lost or build up the church).

LESSON #1

JESUS IS GOD'S WORD

Word: a message of assurance, guarantee, authorization, promise, command, order, creation, or information— conveyed with the intent of being received and acted upon

B
Bible Focus

> *In the beginning was the Word, and the Word was with
> God, and the Word was God. He was in the beginning with
> God. All things were made through Him, and without Him
> nothing was made that was made. In Him was life, and the
> life was the light of men. And the light shines in the dark-
> ness, and the darkness did not comprehend it. . . .*
>
> *He was in the world, and the world was made through
> Him, and the world did not know Him. He came to His own,
> and His own did not receive Him. But as many as received
> Him, to them He gave the right to become children of God,
> to those who believe in His name: who were born, not of
> blood, nor of the will of the flesh, nor of the will of man, but
> of God.*
>
> *And the Word became flesh and dwelt among us, and we
> beheld His glory, the glory as of the only begotten of the
> Father, full of grace and truth.*
>
> *John bore witness of Him and cried out, saying, "This was
> He of whom I said, 'He who comes after me is preferred
> before me, for He was before me.'"*
>
> *And of His fullness we have all received, and grace for
> grace. For the law was given through Moses, but grace and
> truth came through Jesus Christ. No one has seen God at
> any time. The only begotten Son, who is in the bosom of the
> Father, He has declared Him (John 1:1–5, 10–18).*

John's cornerstone of understanding is that words have life-giving meaning. All words flow from a living source of meaning, reflect ongoing
life-related meaning, and produce life-imparting meaning in the minds and
hearts of those who perceive, receive, and believe them.

In a broad and sweeping overview, the longstanding Jewish understanding
of words was this:

Some words are *names*. Names embody the identity of a person—that
person's attributes, personality characteristics, and nature. Names embody
the full and true nature of something. The one whose name is above all
names—Jesus—embodies the full and true nature of God, and therefore, of
all things God created. In this, Jesus *was* and *is* truth.

Some words are *verbs*. They motivate action and compel response. They
have energy and are full of life. Jesus, God's Word spoken into the world,
gave life to the world.

Some words are *adjectives* and *adverbs*. They embody nuances of form, beauty, importance, effectiveness, and understanding. They differentiate good from evil and good from best, and thus, give focus and direction. They are integral to a person's understanding of the true, narrow, life-filled way of God that is best for man to pursue. Jesus was not just a man, He was the Son of God, and was the ultimate revelation of God.

It is no accident that Jesus identified Himself as *the way, the truth, and the life* to His disciples (John 14:6).

The Jew from ancient times also considered words to have importance and some degree of power.

The ancient world regarded the spoken word as a *deed*. They believed spoken words had as much impact as the blow of a hammer or a tender kiss. Jews for thousands of years believed the word uttered from an individual's mouth changed the world. The expulsion of air from the body—in a direction and with a degree of form and energy—impacted the immediate atmosphere surrounding a person and had both a ripple effect and a chain reaction that extended outward. In this way, words took on creative and spiritual power in both the natural and supernatural realms.

Jesus as the Word of God, John said, held all meaning in His being. He embodied the entire nature of God, had the authority and power to implement every desire of God, and was the full revelation of God's love.

Jesus, as God's expression of Himself into the world, created everything—the natural world and the spiritual world. He alone has full authority to create something from nothing, and to transform a sinful man or woman into a forgiven child in right standing with God. He alone is the author of life.

Jesus fully communicated God's plan and purpose for the world, and fully atoned for sins so we might live in a restored and loving relationship with our heavenly Father.

Words are capsules of meaning about who God is, who we are, how to have a relationship with Him, and how best to live in relationship with other people. Jesus was the fullness of meaning in all of these ways. He is the ultimate embodiment—the incarnation—of God. Jesus is the ultimate man, reflecting who we become as we allow the Holy Spirit of God to indwell us and to work in and through us. He is the ultimate embodiment of how to live in constant, intimate relationship with God the Father and God the Holy Spirit. Jesus is the ultimate expression of how we are to live in relationship with others.

One of the great mysteries and glories of God is that we human beings have been given the gift of language. Our ability to hold memories in the form of words, to convey concepts by means of words, and to express the full depth of our own ideas and feelings in words, sets us apart from all other creatures. It is by our words that we present the Word of God to others. What a tremendous privilege and responsibility we have to convey the Word to the world!

What meaning has Jesus given to *you*?

What identity has Jesus given *you*?

For what purpose has Jesus created *you*? In what ways is the word of your life an extension of His Word to *your* world?

In what ways does God call you to speak His Word to those you encounter every day?

A
Application for Today

"Sticks and stones may break my bones, but words will never hurt me."

Most children in the western world have heard that statement, and many have used it in reply to those who have taunted, ridiculed, or criticized them. The statement, however, is far from the truth.

Words can and do inflict pain—sometimes deep emotional, psychological, or spiritual pain. Words can produce tremendous inner turmoil, discouragement, anger, fear, and bitterness.

Consider the impact any one of these statements might have to inflict pain:

"I don't love you anymore."

"You can't do anything right"

"Nothing you do will ever matter or succeed."

"You are stupid."

"I don't want you around—never did, don't now, never will."

Ouch!

Consider the impact repeated expressions such as these might have on a person over time, especially on a young child.

Have you ever been the victim of hurtful words? Have you ever spoken words you know hurt others? How is the pain magnified by the fact that once spoken, words cannot be recalled?

On the flip side . . .

Just as words have the power to hurt, they also have tremendous power to heal, to encourage, to build up, and to reward.

"I love you more than life itself!"

"I can't wait to be with you."

"You are wonderful!"

"You did a fabulous job."

"You deserve the best."

How do you feel when you hear such statements?

Who speaks words of love, encouragement, or reward into your life? How do you feel toward the person who makes such statements?

Do you frequently speak encouraging words? If not, what holds you back?

Not only can words hurt or heal, they have the power to create. Words are at the beginning of virtually all inventions and innovations. What you can express in words often is what can be established in reality. Even words that depict a fantasy often reflect what we suspect may be a possible reality in the distant future, in eternity, or in the unseen spiritual realm.

Given the tremendous power of words, how important is it we choose our words carefully, intentionally, and closely monitor how we speak to others?

What difference might our choice of words have on our ability to convey the gospel of Jesus Christ effectively?

S
Supplementary Scriptures to Consider

The Bible tells us *everything* in our world today was created by God's spoken words:

> In the beginning God created the heavens and the earth. The earth was without form, and void; and darkness was on the face of the deep. And the Spirit of God was hovering over the face of the waters. Then God said . . . Then God saw everything that He had made, and indeed it was very good (Genesis 1:1–3, 31).

- Have you ever been part of a creative process that began with an idea uttered in words?

- How do you respond to the fact that in the first chapter of Genesis, God called everything that He made *good*? Do you believe God has said the same thing about His creation of you?

- In what ways is it important for us to acknowledge that all of our creative ability comes from God?

- In what ways is it important to create those things—and those relationships—that God will call *good*?

According to the Gospel of John, the first miracle of Jesus was a creative miracle, resulting from Jesus speaking:

> On the third day there was a wedding in Cana of Galilee, and the mother of Jesus was there. Now both Jesus and His disciples were invited to the wedding. And when they ran out of wine, the mother of Jesus said to Him, "They have no wine."

Jesus said to her, "Woman, what does your concern have to do with Me? My hour has not yet come."

His mother said to the servants, "Whatever He says to you, do it."

Now there were set there six waterpots of stone, according to the manner of purification of the Jews, containing twenty or thirty gallons apiece. Jesus said to them, "Fill the waterpots with water." And they filled them to the brim. And he said to them, "Draw some out now, and take it to the master of the feast." And they took it. When the master of the feast had tasted the water that was made wine, and did not know where it came from (but the servants who had drawn the water knew), the master of the feast called the bridegroom. And he said to him, "Every man at the beginning sets out the good wine, and when the guests have well drunk, then the inferior. You have kept the good wine until now!" (John 2:1–10)

• Mary wanted Jesus to provide wine in *her* timing. Jesus insisted that He operate on His *own* schedule. How often do we want God to speak to us when we want to hear, or want God to act on our behalf when we want Him to act? What does God do?

• In what ways did Jesus perform this miracle in partnership with human beings? In what ways does God ask us today to be partners in His practical miracles of provision to those who are experiencing need?

- Consider Mary's statement, "Whatever He says to you, do it" (John 2:5). How was this a statement of her faith in Jesus? In what ways are we expressing faith in God—and in others' ability to hear from God—when we say, "Whatever Jesus says to you, do it"?

- Wine at a wedding was a symbol of joy. The more wine, and the better the wine, the greater the joy. In what ways does God command us to create those things that instill joy or cause joy to increase?

God does not speak idle or ineffective words. Everything He has ever spoken, and everything He speaks today, is with intention. His words change us and the world around us:

> "For as the rain comes down, and the snow from heaven,
> And do not return there,
> But water the earth,
> And make it bring forth and bud,
> That it may give seed to the sower
> And bread to the eater,
> So shall My word be that goes forth from My mouth;
> It shall not return to Me void,
> But it shall accomplish what I please,
> And it shall prosper in the thing for which I sent it" (Isaiah 55:10–11).

• Have you ever had something someone said to you stick in your mind and nag at you to the point you finally acted on their words, perhaps long after the words were first spoken? Have you seen this principle at work in the life of another person, perhaps your own child?

• In what ways might you be encouraged by these verses when it comes to words you say in witness to Jesus Christ as the Savior? In what ways is God alone responsible for the impact our words might have on another person's life?

Jesus, who created everything that exists—seen and unseen—is the only human being who ever fully finished anything:

> After this, Jesus, knowing that all things were now accomplished, that the Scripture might be fulfilled, said, "I thirst!" Now a vessel full of sour wine was sitting there; and they filled a sponge with sour wine, put it on hyssop, and put it to His mouth. So when Jesus had received the sour wine, He said, "It is finished!" And bowing His head, He gave up His spirit (John 19:28–30).

In what ways are we each privileged to begin new things—new systems, new organizations or entities, new ministry outreaches? In what ways must we each entrust what we create to God to bring the things we create to fruition or fulfillment?

I
Introspection and Implications

1. What is the most valuable thing you have ever created? How do you feel about your creation?

2. In what ways does everything we create take on a life of its own?

3. What responsibility do you feel for editing something you have said or created? Changing it? Adding to it? Although we can never take back something we have spoken, in what ways can we heal the verbal injuries or rectify the verbal misunderstandings we may have caused?

4. Take stock of your own verbal communication. What would you describe as the main themes? (Think in terms of just one person. What do the two of you talk about most?) How would you describe your overall communication ability (to mean what you say and say what you mean)? Do you talk more than you listen? Is this true of your conversations with God in prayer?

5. Do you see yourself as a creative person? In what ways? Have you underestimated your own creative ability?

C
Communicating the Good News

To a great extent, our sharing the good news of Jesus Christ as Savior and Lord is a matter of getting the Word out. Consider each of the statements below:

- "It doesn't matter how eloquently you talk about Jesus as long as you bring up His name and tell about Him to the best of your ability."

- "The longer and better you know Jesus as Lord, the greater your *vocabulary* when it comes to telling others about Him."

- "Your tone of voice in talking about Jesus says as much as the words you use."

• "A person who really knows—and remains keenly aware of—the saving and forgiving power of Jesus Christ can't help but talk about Him to others who don't know Him."

Do you agree or disagree with these statements? In what ways are you feeling challenged to become a better communicator about your Savior and Lord?

LESSON #2

JESUS IS THE TRUE LIGHT

Light: the primal energy of all creation, the illuminating Source of all that is true

B
Bible Focus

There was a man sent from God, whose name was John. This man came for a witness, to bear witness of the Light, that all through him might believe. He was not that Light, but was sent to bear witness of that Light. That was the true Light which gives light to every man coming into the world (John 1:6–9).

There was a man of the Pharisees named Nicodemus, a ruler of the Jews. This man came to Jesus by night and said to Him, "Rabbi, we know that You are a teacher come from God; for no one can do these signs that You do unless God is with him."

Jesus answered and said to him, "Most assuredly, I say to you, unless one is born again, he cannot see the kingdom of God."

Nicodemus said to Him, "How can a man be born when he is old? Can he enter a second time into his mother's womb and be born?"

Jesus answered, "Most assuredly, I say to you, unless one is born of water and the Spirit, he cannot enter the kingdom of God. That which is born of the flesh is flesh, and that which is born of the Spirit is spirit. Do not marvel that I said to you, 'You must be born again.' The wind blows where it wishes, and you hear the sound of it, but cannot tell where it comes from and where it goes. So is everyone who is born of the Spirit."

Nicodemus answered and said to Him, "How can these things be?"

Jesus answered and said to him, "Are you the teacher of Israel, and do not know these things? Most assuredly, I say to you, We speak what We know and testify what We have seen, and you do not receive Our witness. If I have told you earthly things and you do not believe, how will you believe if I tell you heavenly things? No one has ascended to heaven but He who came down from heaven, that is, the Son of Man who is in heaven. And as Moses lifted up the serpent in the wilderness, even so must the Son of Man be lifted up, that whoever believes in Him should not perish but have eternal life. For God so loved the world that He gave His only begotten Son, that whoever believes in Him should not perish but have

*everlasting life. For God did not send His Son into the world
to condemn the world, but that the world through Him might
be saved.*

*He who believes in Him is not condemned; but he who does
not believe is condemned already, because he has not believed
in the name of the only begotten Son of God. And this is the
condemnation, that the light has come into the world, and men
loved darkness rather than light, because their deeds were
evil. For everyone practicing evil hates the light and does not
come to the light, lest his deeds should be exposed. But he
who does the truth comes to the light, that his deeds may be
clearly seen, that they have been done in God" (John 3:1–21).*

These verses are among the most familiar in the Bible. Consider the
setting of this story. It was customary for Jewish men to meet with other
men in their neighborhood or community during the hours after the evening
meal and before bedtime. This especially was done when a person had a
notable teacher or rabbi as a guest in his home. During these evening hours,
the men studied the Law and the Prophets and engaged in conversations that
focused on the Scriptures and their meaning and application to daily life.
The Jewish day began at sundown, and this practice was a visible outgrowth
of a desire to begin each day focused on the Lord.

Nicodemus came to Jesus *at night* precisely for the purpose of engaging
in a Scripture-based discussion. Nicodemus had been impressed by what He
had heard and seen in Jesus' public ministry. He wanted to know more. In
that, he was not unlike many people today who see miracles or hear sermons
and seek to know more about Christ.

Also like Nicodemus, many people who want to know more about Christ
have preconceptions that stand in their way of receiving or believing the
truth about Christ.

Jesus pointed out that Nicodemus had seen Him in action during the light
of the physical day, but that he hadn't truly understood who Jesus was as the
spiritual light sent from God.

Jesus' conversation with Nicodemus presented three great truths.

First, the spiritual world is the real world.

The Jews had a strong understanding that babies grew in a "watery dark
womb," not unlike the world before God spoke light into being on the first
day of creation. To understand spiritual things, Jesus said, Nicodemus
needed to be spiritually reborn and begin to see with spiritual eyes. He
needed to move from the womb of his preconceptions and enter the real
world of spiritual truth.

How is it possible to do this?

By simply believing in Jesus as the Messiah, the Savior. Jesus reminded Nicodemus of a well-known story in the history of the Israelites. (Look up Numbers 21:4–9.) After a plague of serpents had threatened the camp of the Israelites, the Lord instructed Moses to make a fiery serpent and put it on a pole. The serpent was a symbol of death. However, all who looked upon the serpent with faith that God could and would overcome the serpent with His life-giving power were healed. Jesus clearly said that those who saw Him on a pole of crucifixion—a symbol of death—and *believed* He was God's atoning definitive sacrifice for the sins of the world, would receive everlasting life.

Second, the spiritual realm functions in a way generally opposite to human reasoning.

What was God's motivation for sending Jesus, His only begotten Son, to die for sinful man? Pure and infinite love.

In a few statements, Jesus called Nicodemus to an entirely new approach to life. He presented concepts that were, and are, fundamentally opposite to the way natural man thinks.

We live in a world that says *seeing is believing*. Jesus said, "Believe, and you will see."

The world at large says the physical and material world is the *real* world. Jesus said the *spiritual* world is the *real* world.

The world for the most part says God is punitive. Jesus said God is loving.

The world says good deeds result in reward, and man must *earn* his way to God. Jesus said, "Believing in Me is all that is required for My Father's full acceptance."

Third, people have the capacity to close their eyes and live in a darkness of their own making, even after truth has been revealed to them. They *do* have a choice. Why don't all people *want* to believe and see God's fullness around them? Is it because they don't want to change? They don't want to trade in *their* way for *God's* way. In other words, they don't see because they choose something other than God's plan. They choose to stay in rebellion against God.

To what extent are you willing to change?

To believe before seeing?

To be willing to come into the light of Christ Jesus and walk in His light?

A
Application for Today

Did you have a fear of the dark when you were a child? Most children have some fear of the dark because it represents the great and imminently close unknown. Who might be lurking in the shadows of the night? What might be causing the sounds in the darkness?

How do you feel about being in the dark now that you are an adult? Do you still have a moment of panic when the lights suddenly go out? In what ways do you dislike being *in the dark* figuratively speaking?

If we look closely at *why* we fear the dark, we likely will come face to face with this truth: We trust what we see or otherwise experience by our natural senses. We don't want to take a step unless we can see the ground on which we are about to stand. Seeing results in knowing.

How difficult is it, then to *walk by faith, not by sight*, as Paul wrote to the church at Corinth (2 Corinthians 5:7)?

In what ways do you trust what you can see and distrust what you cannot see?

How comfortable are you with the unknown?

How difficult is it to have faith in those things you cannot prove with your senses?

What does it mean for you to walk by faith in a current situation or circumstance about which you have many questions and few answers?

S
Supplementary Scriptures to Consider

For millennia, darkness has been linked with both ignorance and evil. Light has been linked with understanding and goodness. Keep those concepts in mind as you read these words of Jesus:

> Then Jesus spoke to them again, saying, "I am the light of
> the world. He who follows Me shall not walk in darkness,
> but have the light of life" (John 8:12).

- In what ways has your relationship with Christ Jesus produced greater understanding? Be specific.

- In what ways has your relationship with Christ Jesus allowed you to see evil more clearly, so you might choose what is good?

- Jesus is a light we are to *follow*. How does this relate to your concept of a good role model? What are the benefits of having an example who leads you into greater understanding and goodness?

- Jesus said that in following Him, we would have the light of life. How does a person internalize the Light? Why is it important to *follow* Jesus, not just know about Him?

• What do you believe Jesus would say to those who advocate, "Do as I say, not as I do"?

Jesus confronted one of the main reasons that people do not choose to believe in Him and walk in the Light of His life and teachings:

> Nevertheless even among the rulers many believed in Him, but because of the Pharisees they did not confess Him, lest they should be put out of the synagogue; for they loved the praise of men more than the praise of God.
>
> Then Jesus cried out and said, "He who believes in Me, believes not in Me but in Him who sent Me. And he who sees Me sees Him who sent Me. I have come as a light into the world, that whoever believes in Me should not abide in darkness. And if anyone hears My words, and does not believe, I do not judge him; for I did not come to judge the world, but to save the world. He who rejects Me, and does not receive My words, has that which judges him—the word that I have spoken will judge him in the last day. For I have not spoken on My own authority; but the Father who sent Me gave Me a command, what I should say and what I should speak. And I know that His command is everlasting life. Therefore, whatever I speak, just as the Father has told Me, so I speak" (John 12:42–50).

• Have you ever been reluctant to confess Jesus as your Savior because you were afraid of what *important* people might say about you or do to you?

• What differences do you see between God the Father and God the Son? Are these differences rooted in the roles they fill, or in their nature? Many people seem to fear God and regard Him as judgmental and austere; they often see Jesus as much more loving, approachable, and generally *nicer*. How would Jesus respond to such opinions?

I
Introspection and Implications

1. Is there an area in your life in which you are confused about what is right and wrong, good and evil? How might you clear up that confusion?

2. Is there an issue in your life in which you would like to have greater understanding? How might you gain greater clarity?

3. Have you ever followed someone you thought was a good role model, only to become disillusioned or disappointed? What did you do? Why are we wise to follow Jesus directly as our example who never fails?

4. A man once told his partners in ministry, "Follow me only as long as you can look over my shoulder and see Jesus." How might we each benefit from adopting this approach in our relationships with those who are under our authority?

5. Have you ever experienced a spiritual *Aha!* moment when suddenly the Holy Spirit seemed to bring you greater meaning about a Bible passage? Why is it important to ask the Holy Spirit to guide your reading of the Bible? Why is it important for you to seek confirmation of any revelation or insight you have into God's truth?

6. After you accepted Jesus Christ as your Savior, did you find you needed to set aside some preconceptions about God the Father, God the Son, or God the Holy Spirit?

C
Communicating the Good News

Does the story of Nicodemus give you hope that God will reveal the truth about Jesus to any person who is honestly searching for the truth about how to have a closer relationship with God?

In your own words, how do you explain what it means to be *born again*? What is *our* part in being born again? What is *God's* part?

How important is it that we require a person to simply *believe* in Jesus Christ to be born again? How important is it that we require people to actively believe in Jesus Christ to be born again, rather than maintaining that since the moment Jesus died on the cross, He automatically saves every person who is born? This is a major tenet of universalism, a philosophy rampant in our world today.

How important is it that we take Jesus at His word that *whosoever will believe* means *whosoever*?

LESSON #3

JESUS IS THE BREAD OF LIFE FROM HEAVEN

Bread: the staple of life—all that is needed to sustain a life of wholeness

B
Bible Focus

daily Bread

On the following day, when the people who were standing on the other side of the sea saw that there was no other boat there, except that one which His disciples had entered, and that Jesus had not entered the boat with His disciples, but His disciples had gone away alone—however, other boats came from Tiberias, near the place where they ate bread after the Lord had given thanks—when the people therefore saw that Jesus was not there, nor His disciples, they also got into boats and came to Capernaum, seeking Jesus. And when they found Him on the other side of the sea, they said to Him, "Rabbi, when did You come here?"

Jesus answered them and said, "Most assuredly, I say to you, you seek Me, not because you saw the signs, but because you ate of the loaves and were filled. Do not labor for the food which perishes, but for the food which endures to everlasting life, which the Son of Man will give you, because God the Father has set His seal on Him."

Then they said to Him, "What shall we do, that we may work the works of God?"

Jesus answered and said to them, "This is the work of God, that you believe in Him whom He sent."

Therefore they said to Him, "What sign will You perform then, that we may see it and believe You? What work will You do? Our fathers ate the manna in the desert; as it is written, 'He gave them bread from heaven to eat.'"

Then Jesus said to them, "Most assuredly, I say to you, Moses did not give you the bread from heaven, but My Father gives you the true bread from heaven. For the bread of God is He who comes down from heaven and gives life to the world."

Then they said to Him, "Lord, give us this bread always."

And Jesus said to them, "I am the bread of life. He who comes to Me shall never hunger, and he who believes in Me shall never thirst. But I said to you that you have seen Me and yet do not believe. All that the Father gives Me will come to Me, and the one who comes to Me I will by no means cast out. For I have come down from heaven, not to do My own will, but the will of Him who sent Me. This is the will of the Father who sent Me, that of all He has given Me I should lose nothing, but should raise it up at the last day. And this is the will

of Him who sent Me, that everyone who sees the Son and
believes in Him may have everlasting life; and I will raise him
up at the last day" (John 6:22–40).

In the days of Moses, the Israelites were given manna as their source of
nutrition as they wandered in the wilderness between Egypt and the Land of
Promise (Exodus 16:4–5). The gathering of manna was daily, with a double
portion gathered on the day before the Sabbath and no manna gathered on
the Sabbath. God's provision for the Israelites was practical, sufficient, and
easily acquired. His provision was given to them because they were His
beloved people, despite their disobedience at times.

God's miraculous free-flowing provision was deeply etched in the Jewish
soul. At the same time, the constraints and taxes of Rome were ominous and
ever present to those who encountered Jesus on a Galilee hillside. It's
difficult, therefore, to fault those who were given portions of bread and fish
on the day Jesus multiplied a boy's lunch to feed five thousand men and
their families! Jesus seemed to be providing bread that was sufficient and
easily acquired. What a good life to listen to Jesus teach all day, eat a free
meal in the late afternoon, and then sleep under the stars until the teaching
began the next day!

The people were eager to follow Jesus and experience the easy life He
offered, but they missed the point. Jesus was illustrating far greater truths in
His miracle. He was expressing the reality that God cares that our daily
needs are met, and He often provides ways for us to have our needs met in
ways we have not imagined or pursued. Jesus was also teaching by example
the eternal truth that He is the source of true spiritual nourishment. He alone
satisfies. Jesus is the bread from heaven that provides all a person needs for
spiritual wholeness (John 6:32).

The people who sought out Jesus that day were not unlike many people
today who want a relationship with God solely because of what they think
God will do for them as they live day-to-day in this natural, material world.
How many people do you know who turn to God . . .

- only when they need a miracle of healing or provision?

- because they think He is going to create for them a life without problems or troubles?

- because it seems like a socially advantageous thing to do to join the
  church where their neighbors, friends, or people at work attend?

- hoping He will fulfill their dreams, which lie far beyond their needs?

How often do people turn away from God because He hasn't lived up to their expectations?

God's call to us is always a call to relationship—one that is for every moment of every day, and then for all eternity. God's invitation to us is to seek first the spiritual realm, and then to trust Him to show us how and when and where He has made provision for our material needs. His means of provision often involves old-fashioned work.

Every Christian perhaps struggles to some degree with the reason they love God. Do you love God because He is lovable? Because He loved you first? Because of His blessings? Because it is commanded?

In what ways has God shown His love to you regardless of your behavior or emotions toward Him?

A
Application for Today

The sign in the restaurant said in large letters, "We serve slow food, not fast food." In smaller type were these words: "We spend hours preparing our meats by a slow-cook method. We take hours to chop up the freshest ingredients to make our salads every day. We bake our own bread and make our own desserts. We have only three employees to take your order, put together your order in the kitchen, and serve you. If you have the time, we'll provide for you a great meal. If you don't have the time, come back. We're worth waiting for. But no, we can't 'hurry it up' on demand."

The restaurant does a steady business, but it will never become a franchised chain or serve hundreds of people a day. It is too slow to jockey for position in life's fast lane.

We live in a world that demands immediate gratification at every turn!

We want fast food, even though we prefer the taste of *slow* food.

We seem irresistibly drawn as a culture to purchase lottery tickets and pursue get-rich-quick schemes. We admire and desire overnight success.

We want to earn academic degrees in less and less time, regardless of what is or isn't learned.

We want to get something right the first time we try it.

We want to fall in love at first sight and if things don't work out, get a quick divorce at a low cost.

We want wars to end forty-eight hours after they are started, crimes to be resolved in real life at the pace of a prime-time television show, and to have at age twenty all it took our parents or grandparents a lifetime to acquire.

What about our spiritual life?

How long should it take for a person to become spiritually mature?

How long should it take for God to answer your prayer?

How long should a preacher preach or a teacher teach? How long should a church service last?

How long is *long enough* to spend reading your Bible?

How long is *long enough* to pray?

S
Supplementary Scriptures to Consider

Jesus elaborated on His teaching about Himself as the Bread of Life:

The Jews then complained about Him, because He said, "I am the bread which came down from heaven." And they said, "Is not this Jesus, the son of Joseph, whose father and mother we know? How is it then that He says, 'I have come down from heaven'?"

Jesus therefore answered and said to them, "Do not murmur among yourselves. No one can come to Me unless the Father who sent Me draws him; and I will raise him up at the last day. It is written in the prophets, 'And they shall all be taught by God.' Therefore everyone who has heard and learned from the Father comes to Me. Not that anyone has seen the Father, except He who is from God; He has seen the Father. Most assuredly, I say to you, he who believes in Me has everlasting life. I am the bread of life. Your fathers ate the manna in the wilderness, and are dead. This is the bread which comes down from heaven, that one may eat of it and not die. I am the living bread which came down from heaven. If anyone eats of this bread, he will live forever; and the bread that I shall give is My flesh, which I shall give for the life of the world."

The Jews therefore quarreled among themselves, saying, "How can this Man give us His flesh to eat?"

Then Jesus said to them, "Most assuredly, I say to you, unless you eat the flesh of the Son of Man and drink His blood, you have no life in you. Whoever eats My flesh and drinks My blood has eternal life, and I will raise him up at the last day. For My flesh is food indeed, and My blood is drink indeed. He who eats My flesh and drinks My blood abides in Me, and I in him. As the living Father sent Me, and I live because of the Father, so he who feeds on Me will live because of Me. This is the bread which came down from heaven—not as your fathers ate the manna, and are dead. He who eats this bread will live forever" (John 6:41–58).

- In your own words, how do you explain what it means to *eat* the bread of Jesus' life?

- Have you ever explained the partaking of communion elements (bread and wine) to someone who has never viewed or experienced this practice in the church? What did you say? What questions did they ask? If you haven't tried to explain communion to an unbeliever or a new believer, how might you describe it? What questions might you anticipate?

- Bread in the ancient world was usually baked daily, and intended to be consumed daily. What is the difference between things we do for short-term benefit and things we do for long-term benefit? (Examples: investments, health-related habits) What does it mean for something we do now to have eternal benefit?

- Do we behave differently when we think something is only for the short term and not the long term of life?

- Do we tend to place higher value on things that bring immediate reward, or things that hold potential for a longer and more lasting reward?

I

Introspection and Implications

1. What things do you believe are the bare essentials for you to live a good life?

2. What percentage of your time and effort in any given day is devoted to things related to short-term activities, goals, and rewards? What percentage of your time and effort is devoted to things related to long-range goals and rewards? What percentage of your time and effort on any given day is devoted to things that God says are eternal?

3. What percentage of your money is spent on daily living? What percentage of your material treasure do you set aside for the long term or for eternal benefit?

4. What kind of *Jesus eater* are you? Do you nibble? Gobble? Come to Him with a ravenous appetite to consume all His life? Are you a picky eater—choosing the parts about Jesus that you like and leaving the rest untouched? Do you expect Jesus to force-feed you? Provide His life to you intravenously?

5. What do you consider to be the basics for good spiritual nutrition?

C
Communicating the Good News

"How may I help you?" That question is the heart and soul of customer service. Is it also at the heart of sharing the gospel?

In what ways are we to *feed* others the Bread of Life in a form and at a pace they can digest what is given to them?

LESSON #4

JESUS IS THE GOOD SHEPHERD

*Shepherd: one who has full authority
over the sheep assigned to him, and who is
one hundred percent responsible for the total
well-being of the sheep under his care*

B
Bible Focus

> Then Jesus said to them again, "Most assuredly, I say to
> you, I am the door of the sheep. All who ever came before Me
> are thieves and robbers, but the sheep did not hear them. I am
> the door. If anyone enters by Me, he will be saved, and will go
> in and out and find pasture. The thief does not come except to
> steal, and to kill, and to destroy. I have come that they may
> have life, and that they may have it more abundantly.
>
> "I am the good shepherd. The good shepherd gives His life
> for the sheep. But a hireling, he who is not the shepherd, one
> who does not own the sheep, sees the wolf coming and leaves
> the sheep and flees; and the wolf catches the sheep and
> scatters them. The hireling flees because he is a hireling and
> does not care about the sheep. I am the good shepherd; and I
> know My sheep, and am known by My own. As the Father
> knows Me, even so I know the Father; and I lay down My life
> for the sheep. And other sheep I have which are not of this
> fold; them also I must bring, and they will hear My voice; and
> there will be one flock and one shepherd.
>
> "Therefore My Father loves Me, because I lay down My life
> that I may take it again. No one takes it from Me, but I lay it
> down of Myself. I have power to lay it down, and have power
> to take it again. This command I have received from My
> Father" (John 10:7–18).

Most Americans today know little about sheepherding in the Middle East.
Four principles associated with sheepherding add significantly to our understanding of what Jesus taught about being the Good Shepherd.

First, shepherds *lead* their sheep. They do not prod the sheep from behind
or use dogs to keep them on the right path. The sheep follow the sound of
the shepherd's voice as he leads them to safe pastures and still waters.

Second, shepherds *know* their sheep and routinely call them by name.
Sheep are raised primarily for wool, and unless a newborn lamb is ear-
marked at birth for sacrifice, or for later family feasting, a sheep is given a
name and nurtured almost as a beloved pet.

Third, sheep pens are often hillside caves, especially in the area of Bethle-
hem. When a pen is constructed in an open field, it is usually made of thorny
brush piled high with no roof and an open space as a doorway. The shepherd
himself lies in the open doorway at night to fend off any would-be predators.

Fourth, shepherds are those who *own* their sheep or are the children of flock owners. *Hirelings* are hired hands who work for wages and generally have no long-term relationship with the sheep or benefit from the flock. Shepherds, who consider the sheep not only their livelihood but as being almost part of their families, sometimes do lose their own lives while protecting their flocks from ravaging wolves, wild dogs, or mountain lions. A hireling rarely has such a deeply vested interest in keeping his job.

For millennia before Jesus, the Jewish people had a strong understanding that God the Father was the *Great Shepherd.* Psalm 23, which begins "The LORD is my shepherd," is perhaps the most famous of all the psalms. Jesus was making a direct *God* statement in referring to Himself as the Great Shepherd.

A number of the prophets referred to God's shepherding of the Israelites— leading His people to provision, protecting them against all forms of evil, and loving them in a personal way. Here are just a few well-known references:

> *All we like sheep have gone astray;*
> *We have turned, every one, to his own way;*
> *And the LORD has laid on Him the iniquity of us all (Isaiah 53:6).*

> *"Woe to the shepherds who destroy and scatter the sheep of My pasture!" says the LORD. Therefore thus says the LORD God of Israel against the shepherds who feed My people: "You have scattered My flock, driven them away, and not attended to them. Behold, I will attend to you for the evil of your doings," says the LORD. "But I will gather the remnant of My flock out of all countries where I have driven them, and bring them back to their folds; and they shall be fruitful and increase. I will set up shepherds over them who will feed them; and they shall fear no more, nor be dismayed, nor shall they be lacking," says the LORD (Jeremiah 23:1–4).*

> *"My people have been lost sheep.*
> *Their shepherds have led them astray;*
> *They have turned them away on the mountains.*
> *They have gone from mountain to hill;*
> *They have forgotten their resting place.*
> *All who found them have devoured them;*
> *And their adversaries said, 'We have not offended,*
> *Because they have sinned against the LORD, the habitation of justice,*
> *The LORD, the hope of their fathers'" (Jeremiah 50:6–7).*

The prophets made it clear that the Lord would seek out His sheep and provide godly leadership for them. Jesus, of course, was not only speaking to His disciples, but to Pharisees who had been critical of Him and had engaged in a debate about their own authority and righteousness. The Pharisees knew the words of the prophets. They understood fully and clearly Jesus was calling their leadership into question.

Jesus made it clear that shepherds exist for the benefit of the sheep. The Pharisees had come to a point where they believed the sheep existed for their benefit.

Jesus called the people back to the original understanding of the Old Testament: to be a shepherd was to be a servant. To be the Great Shepherd was to be the Supreme Servant. Not that God existed to do the bidding of His children, but rather, that God—in His everlasting love—was motivated to serve, help, nourish, nurture, protect, and provide for His children. The job of the sheep is to follow and obey; God's job is to lead.

To be a *shepherd* of God's people today always means authority is coupled with tremendous responsibility for the welfare of the sheep.

We live in a power-hungry and prestige-craved world. How many people want power over the masses below them, or seek adoring prestige of the fans who follow them, but do not want any responsibility for the well-being of those who flock to them? How many desire their subordinates and underlings to give to them or do for them, and never give a thought to ways they might serve those under their leadership?

How true is this in some churches or ministry organizations?

What would Jesus say?

A
Application for Today

The story is told of a best-selling novelist who wrote a letter to a friend, saying, "Have you heard the one about the novelist who met an old friend? After they had talked for two hours, the novelist said, 'Now we've talked about me long enough—let's talk about you! What did *you* think of my last novel?" [1]

We live in an it-is-all-about-me world!

To what extent do you expect others to serve you? Do you assume this of those in authority over you? Do you expect this of others who are under your

---

[[1]*Note:* Novelist was Elizabeth Chevalier, author of *Driven Woman*, writing to Macmillan. Anecdote found in Paul Lee Tan, editor, *Encyclopedia of 7,700 Illustrations*, Dallas, TX: Bible Communications, Inc., 1996]

supervision or authority? To what extent are you willing to serve those under you? Those over you?

Who is listening to the sound of *your* voice and following what you have to say?

How responsible do you feel for that person or that group of people? Would you give your life for that person or group?

S
Supplementary Scriptures to Consider

Perhaps the most famous passage of Scripture in the Old Testament speaks about the role of the Great Shepherd:

> The LORD is my shepherd;
> I shall not want.
> He makes me to lie down in green pastures;
> He leads me beside the still waters.
> He restores my soul;
> He leads me in the paths of righteousness
> For His name's sake.
>   Yea, though I walk through the valley of the shadow of
>   death,
> I will fear no evil;
> For You are with me;
> Your rod and Your staff, they comfort me (Psalm 23:1–4).

• How does the shepherd in this psalm provide for all the sheep's needs? Consider the relationship between the emotional and spiritual needs represented by the phrases *restores my soul, leads me in the paths of righteousness for His name's sake, fear no evil,* and, *You are with me.*

- Shepherds used the rod to ward off predators. The staff had a crook at one end and was used to rescue a sheep fallen into a rocky crevice or down a slippery slope. In what ways has the Lord warded off evil on your behalf? In what ways has the Lord rescued you from the consequences of your own error or bad judgment?

Jesus further explained the relationship He had as Shepherd with His sheep:

> Now it was the Fast of Dedication in Jerusalem, and it was winter. And Jesus walked in the temple, in Solomon's porch. Then the Jews surrounded Him and said to Him, "How long do You keep us in doubt? If You are the Christ, tell us plainly."
>
> Jesus answered them, "I told you, and you do not believe. The works that I do in My Father's name, they bear witness of Me. But you do not believe, because you are not of My sheep, as I said to you. My sheep hear My voice, and I know them, and they follow Me. And I give them eternal life, and they shall never perish, neither shall anyone snatch them out of My hand. My Father, who has given them to Me, is greater than all; and no one is able to snatch them out of My Father's hand. I and My Father are one" (John 10:22–30).

- Have you ever had an experience where you believed and obeyed the Lord without *fully* understanding all He was saying to you, calling you to do, or asking you to give? What were the results?

• Reflect on Jesus' statement, "My sheep hear My voice, and I know them, and they follow Me" (John 10:27). How do you hear the Lord's voice? What comfort do you take in Jesus' phrase, "I know them. . . I give them eternal life, and they shall never perish, neither shall anyone snatch them out of My hand" (John 10:27–28)?

• What is the relationship between following the Shepherd and receiving all He offers to the sheep?

Even loyal sheep sometimes stray. The good news is Jesus forgives anything we do that puts distance between God and ourselves, if we are willing to return to following Him. Certainly the apostle Peter knew that well!

> Peter said to Him, "Lord, why can I not follow You now? I will lay down my life for your sake."
> Jesus answered him, "Will you lay down your life for My sake? Most assuredly, I say to you, the rooster shall not crow till you have denied Me three times" (John 13:37–38).

Read John 18:15–17 and 18:25–27. Peter did deny Jesus three times before dawn. After the crucifixion and resurrection, Peter returned to Galilee to fish and Jesus encountered him and other disciples there. Jesus gave Peter a three-fold opportunity to affirm his love:

> So when they had eaten breakfast, Jesus said to Simon Peter, "Simon, son of Jonah, do you love Me more than these?"

He said to Him, "Yes, Lord; You know that I love You."
He said to him, "Feed My lambs."
He said to him again a second time, "Simon, son of Jonah, do you love Me?"
He said to Him, "Yes, Lord; You know that I love You."
He said to him, "Tend My sheep."
He said to him the third time, "Simon, son of Jonah, do you love Me?" Peter was grieved because He said to him the third time, "Do you love Me?"
And he said to Him, "Lord, You know all things; You know that I love You."
Jesus said to him, "Feed My sheep" (John 21:15–17).

- Have you ever strayed from following the Good Shepherd, Jesus? How did the Lord deal with you? In what ways did the Lord give you an opportunity to reaffirm your faith in Him and love for Him?

- The Lord challenged the fisherman Peter to become the shepherd Peter. How do the three aspects of shepherding differ from one another?
    Feed Christ's lambs.
    Tend Christ's sheep.
    Feed Christ's sheep.
    What are the implications of this challenge to you in the ministry to which God has called you?

I
Introspection and Implications

1. Every person seems to hear the Shepherd's voice in a personal way. How do you explain to another person that you have *heard* the Lord speak to you? How do you verify in your own heart and mind that you have heard from the Lord—and that what you heard wasn't a figment of your own imagination?

2. Every person seems to be led by the Shepherd in slightly different ways. How do you experience God's *leading* you into new challenges or opportunities? Do you ask questions as part of receiving God's direction? If so, what are the foremost questions you ask? How do you receive God's answers to your questions?

3. Have you ever blamed God for leading you astray or for allowing something bad to happen to you? Was it truly the Lord leading you, or were you in rebellion? Were you listening to a voice other than the Lord's?

4. What do you say to people who want God to do for them and give to them, but have no desire to do for or give to God?

5. Why do people prefer to lead their own lives rather than follow the Good Shepherd?

C
Communicating the Good News

How would you explain Isaiah 53:6 to a person who does not know the Lord? [All we like sheep have gone astray; We have turned, every one, to his own way; And the LORD has laid on Him the iniquity of us all (Isaiah 53:6).]

What are the foremost benefits of following Jesus as our Good Shepherd?

LESSON #5

JESUS IS THE LIFE-GIVER

The Way: path, direction, line of connection
from before-the-beginning to everlasting-ending
The Truth: the absolute content of eternal reality
The Life: now and forever, alive

B
Bible Focus

> *So when Jesus came, He found that he [Lazarus] had
> already been in the tomb four days. Now Bethany was near
> Jerusalem, about two miles away. And many of the Jews had
> joined the women around Martha and Mary, to comfort them
> concerning their brother.*
>
> *Now Martha, as soon as she heard that Jesus was coming,
> went and met Him, but Mary was sitting in the house. Now
> Martha said to Jesus, "Lord, if You had been here, my brother
> would not have died. But even now I know that whatever You
> ask of God, God will give You."*
>
> *Jesus said to her, "Your brother will rise again."*
>
> *Martha said to Him, "I know that he will rise again in the
> resurrection at the last day."*
>
> *Jesus said to her, "I am the resurrection and the life. He
> who believes in Me, though he may die, he shall live. And
> whoever lives and believes in Me shall never die. Do you
> believe this?"*
>
> *She said to Him, "Yes, Lord, I believe that You are the
> Christ, the Son of God, who is to come into the world" (John
> 11:17–27).*

Jewish tradition at the time of this miracle taught that a deceased person's
soul hovered over the body for up to three days after death. However untrue,
this superstition was widely believed. The fact that Lazarus had been dead
for four days left little doubt in the minds of those comforting Martha and
Mary that Lazarus was definitively, irreversibly, and undeniably dead.

When Martha went out to meet Jesus, she affirmed her faith in Him, even
as she voiced her disappointment that He had not come earlier. She still
believed He had power to heal, and to have God the Father hear and answer
His prayers, but she had no hope Jesus would restore her brother to life
anytime soon. She even misunderstood Jesus' statement that her brother
would rise again. She saw this as a future event, not an immediate one.

In speaking to Martha, and then in speaking to Lazarus and calling him
from the tomb, Jesus was making a bold affirmation of His deity: He had the
ability to call things that are definitively, irreversibly, and undeniably dead
back to life! God alone gives and governs life, and in so doing, governs the
boundaries of death.

Believing Jesus has this ability is the cornerstone of our hope that He will

LESSON #5 • Jesus Is the Life-Giver **61**

one day call us from physical death into eternal life with Him. The coroner or physician may pronounce you *dead*, but Jesus says, "You will live . . . forever!" What tremendous hope this gives to every person who calls Jesus Savior and Lord!

One of the great lessons we can learn from Martha is that regardless of what happens to us, or to others we love, we must hold on to our faith that Jesus can heal, restore, reconcile, and deliver even in the most difficult of circumstances. We may not experience the miracle we want, but that does not mean God has lost any of His miracle-working power. His timing, His methods, and His purposes are often beyond our ability to perceive or understand.

We must also see this miracle in the broader context of all things that seem to be definitively, irreversibly, or undeniably dead, lost, or gone. How many Christians around the world today are facing the specter of tremendous loss? Some are estranged from a spouse, parent, or friend. Some have lost their health, and some have lost a once-good relationship with a child who is now pursuing a path of sin. Sometimes the loss involves a long-standing job, a family estate or farm, or an office or position. Some people are facing the loss of their ability to live on their own or travel at will, and in some nations, people are facing a loss of their freedom to speak openly about Jesus or to worship Him in public gatherings.

What hope does the story of Lazarus give you about those situations that seem totally without life or beyond hope? Do you trust Jesus to be the resurrection and life-giving force for the relationship that seems to be definitively, irreversibly, or undeniably dead? Do you trust Jesus to be the life-restorer of what appears to be gone or lost forever?

Jesus called Lazarus to "come forth!" And when Jesus called, Lazarus came forth! He was "bound hand and foot with grave clothes, and his face was wrapped with a cloth." Jesus said, "Loose him, and let him go" (John 11:43–44).

Jesus calls people every day to *come forth* from their old lives and to live a new life in Him. He rescues sinners from the pit they're in. He gives everlasting life to those who have been pursing everlasting death. A challenge we each face as Christians is to *loose* those new believers in Christ Jesus. We must help them shed the remnants of their *life of death* and put on a new perspective and new habits. We must help them live in freedom.

It is not enough just to be resurrected. We must embrace the life to which we have been raised. Jesus did not simply claim to be the resurrection. He laid claim to being life itself. It is not enough that we turn from the sin that leads to everlasting death, but to pursue all Jesus calls us to be and do with our whole hearts.

A
Application for Today

In Tewin churchyard, close to King's Cross Station, one of the largest trees in England grows from a grave identified as that of Lady Anne Grimston. The tree is a monument to life, and also a reminder of God's resurrection power.

Lady Anne Grimston did not believe in life after death. As she was dying in her palatial home, she said with great cynicism to a friend, "I shall live again as surely as a tree will grow from my body." She was buried in a marble tomb and her grave was marked by a large marble slab and surrounded by an iron railing. Years later, someone discovered that the marble slab appeared to have moved a little. Then it cracked, and through the crack, a small tree began to grow. As the tree continued to grow, its trunk eventually tore apart the iron railing and shattered the marble slab, and the tomb became engulfed by the tree's massive roots.

It doesn't really matter what we conclude about the extent of God's power. His power is absolute and infinite. There is nothing we can do to control God, stop God, or cause God to act as we want Him to act. What we *can* do is line up our lives with God's plan and purpose. We can choose to put our faith in what God can do and what God says He will do, rather than discount His Word or dismiss it as invalid.

We do not give life to God. He gives life to us.

We cannot fully control the trajectory of any relationship, career, or ministry effort. Only God determines the outcome of seeds we plant and the faith we voice.

We bury the dead. God raises the dead.

In what ways are you challenged to trust God to resurrect something in your personal life, family, or church?

S
Supplementary Scriptures to Consider

Jesus made a bold *I am* statement that He encompassed and embodied all of life—its answers and solutions (truth), its direction and definitions (way), and its energy (life):

> [Jesus said,] "Let not your heart be troubled; you believe in God, believe also in Me. In My Father's house are many mansions; if it were not so, I would have told you. I go to prepare a place for you. And if I go and prepare a place for you, I will come again and receive you to Myself; that where

I am, there you may be also. And where I go you know, and the way you know."

Thomas said to Him, "Lord, we do not know where You are going, and how can we know the way?"

Jesus said to him, "I am the way, the truth, and the life. No one comes to the Father except through Me" (John 14:1–6).

- In what ways has Jesus called you repeatedly throughout your life to the next place He has prepared for you? How does your recognition of Him being the Way, Truth, and Life help you believe He is preparing the ultimate eternal place for you?

- Many people feel a need for one of these three things right now: answers or solutions that are sure; direction about what to do next; or the strength, energy, and courage to take action. Do you have one of these needs? How are you relying on Jesus to meet your needs?

- A preacher once said, "No matter what question you ask, the answer is 'the Holy Spirit whom Jesus sent.'" Reflect on this statement regarding a particular question or need you have.

• How can we trust Jesus to be Way, Truth, and Life for us in a world in which people are encouraging us to trust virtually everything and everyone but God to yield answers and solutions, give us guidance and standards, and motivate us to succeed?

• Reflect on Jesus' statement, "No one comes to the Father except through Me" (John 14:6). What do you say to a person who claims there are many ways to God the Father apart from belief in Jesus as Savior?

Jesus linked His ongoing life-giving power to our love and obedience:

> [Jesus said,] "If you love Me, keep My commandments. And I will pray the Father, and He will give you another Helper, that He may abide with you forever—the Spirit of truth, whom the world cannot receive, because it neither sees Him nor knows Him; but you know Him, for He dwells with you and will be in you. I will not leave you orphans; I will come to you" (John 14:15–18).
>
> [Jesus said,] "If anyone loves Me, he will keep My word; and My Father will love him, and We will come to him and make Our home with him. He who does not love Me does not keep My words; and the word which you hear is not Mine, but the Father's who sent Me" (John 14:23–24).

Have you experienced an increase in God's life-giving power as you have obeyed Christ's commandments? In what ways? How are your obedience to and love for Christ Jesus linked?

I
Introspection and Implications

1. Do you fear death? In what ways does a strong belief in Christ's resurrection power overcome a fear of death?

2. Is there anything you believe to be beyond God's resurrecting power? Why or why not?

3. Reflect on Jesus' statements, "I will not leave you orphans" (John 14:18) and "Where I go you know, and the way you know" (John 14:4). How does the Holy Spirit within you give you comfort and guidance? Are the two linked? In other words, do you perceive you have the Holy Spirit's guidance when you feel at peace about a decision or feel peace within a situation?

4. A Bible teacher once said, "The Holy Spirit enables us to know Jesus, and when we know Jesus, we know in any situation or circumstance what Jesus would say, how Jesus would respond, what Jesus would do, how He would do it, and ultimately why He would do it." Has this been your experience as you have sought to follow Jesus as the Lord of your life? Be specific. In what ways do you believe experiencing the fullness of the life Jesus offers us is directly related to our being obedient to the Holy Spirit who dwells within us?

C
Communicating the Good News

We often talk about the *walking wounded* or the *walking dead*. In what ways are those who are hurting the worst, or who are feeling the greatest discouragement and despair, the people who are the most open to hearing what we have to say about Jesus?

What is the good news you have to share with a person who is in great pain or is deeply depressed? Are you wise to share this news in words alone? Deeds alone? Actions and words combined? How can you discern what to do, when, and how?

In what ways do you rely on the Holy Spirit to show you how to impart life-giving hope to others around you?

Lesson #6

JESUS IS THE VINE

Abide: to reside within; to remain
within and be totally dependent on

B
Bible Focus

> [Jesus said,] "I am the true vine, and My Father is the
> vinedresser. Every branch in Me that does not bear fruit He
> takes away; and every branch that bears fruit He prunes, that
> it may bear more fruit. You are already clean because of the
> word which I have spoken to you. Abide in Me, and I in you.
> As the branch cannot bear fruit of itself, unless it abides in the
> vine, neither can you, unless you abide in Me.
>
> "I am the vine, you are the branches. He who abides in Me,
> and I in him, bears much fruit; for without Me you can do
> nothing. If anyone does not abide in Me, he is cast out as a
> branch and is withered; and they gather them and throw them
> into the fire, and they are burned. If you abide in Me, and My
> words abide in you, you will ask what you desire, and it shall
> be done for you. By this My Father is glorified, that you bear
> much fruit; so you will be My disciples (John 15:1–8).

The vine is one of the foremost symbols of the nation of Israel, and from
Old Testament days, Israel was called the *vineyard* of God. The psalmist
compared God's people to a vine that had been brought out of Egypt and
planted in the Land of Promise. (See Psalm 80:8.)

Again and again, the prophets called the people to be fruitful and to
remain faithful to God as their husbandman, so their fruit might not be
ravaged by foreign invaders . . . and so the Lord might not destroy His own
vineyard. (See Isaiah 5:1–7.) Fruitfulness and faithfulness are vitally linked
throughout the Old Testament, and Jesus also made this connection. To be
supremely fruitful, Jesus said, a person must be utterly faithful—a branch
must *abide* in the vine at all times. The unfaithful are unfruitful, and are
eventually cut away and destroyed.

But faithful in what ways?

The Pharisees and religious leaders of Jesus' day were certainly faithful in
keeping rituals and various laws associated with their religion. Jesus made it
clear to His disciples that He is the *true vine* (John 15:1). Being faithful, He
said, is not a matter of being faithful to a *what*—a set of laws or rituals—but
faithful to a *who*. Being faithful means being in relationship with God, not
simply attending religious services or going through religious ceremonies.
Jesus made it clear He was and is the *true vine*. The relationship He offers is
living, and it is meaningful. It produces fruit, and that fruit, in turn, gives
life.

"If you abide in Me," Jesus said, "and My words abide in you, you will ask what you desire, and it shall be done for you" (John 15:7). You will live in the fullness of a relationship with God that produces an effective, successful, desirable, fulfilling, satisfying life.

What does it mean for a branch to abide in the vine? To *abide* means *to rest within* and *to be utterly dependent on.* The core stump of a grapevine is the fountain of the vine's life-giving, fruit-producing sap. To abide as a branch in a vine means the branch retains an open and unhindered connection to the core stump. This allows the core stump to push sap through the branch and produce fruit.

What does it mean for us to abide in Jesus? It means to put our faith fully in Jesus, to be utterly dependent on Him in all things, and to do only what He commands us to do by the power of His Holy Spirit. It means to obey God's Word—not allowing ourselves to be compromised by the world's negative or tempting words—so we remain open and unhindered in our ability to receive all the Holy Spirit imparts to us.

One thing every vineyard owner knows is that pruning and fruitfulness are vitally linked. After every harvest season, vines are pruned back so the core stump of the vine can push fruit-producing sap through new supple growth rather than old woody tissue.

How important it is for us to remain *fresh* in our relationship with the Lord at all times! We must not seek to live on yesterday's faith, last year's insights into God's Word, or last decade's miracles. God's mercies are imparted to us new every morning and we must avail ourselves continually of God's fresh new insights into the Scriptures and new promptings about what we are to say, do, and be in our world. (See Lamentations 3:23.)

In ancient times, and in many vineyards in the Middle East today, vines do not grow on trellises or have the support of stakes. Each plant grows freestanding and close to the ground. If a vine stump is not pruned, the branches can grow to great lengths and become entangled or ensnared with other plants or obstacles or be trampled on. The metaphor was obvious to those who heard Jesus. Without *pruning*, it is easy to get caught up in the unimportant, become sidetracked by a competing good idea, or trampled by jealous competitors.

God the Father prunes us by His Word. When we allow the words of Jesus to fill our minds, His teachings become our perspective, our worldview, our habitual way of thinking and feeling, our attitude, and our impetus to act. As this happens, we find we know with certainty what to say, and what to do—and just as importantly, what to cut away from our lives and our imaginations.

Are you bearing *much fruit* in your world today? Is it life-giving fruit?

Are you faithfully abiding in Jesus, the True Vine?

Are you trusting the Holy Spirit to work in you, and through you, daily?

Are you asking the Lord to help you remain single-hearted in your focus on Him so you might clearly hear His directives and receive His power?

A
Application for Today

"I got up this morning," the person said, "fully intending to spend some time with the Lord and read my Bible, but first I decided to brush my teeth, run a comb through my hair, and start the coffee pot. The dog was eager to be let out, so I took the opportunity to pick up the newspaper on the front lawn, and a headline captured my attention. I read the paper until the coffee was ready and then let the dog in, and as I stood by the door, I realized the plants on the stand there needed a little water. After I watered the plants, and mopped up the water I spilled in the process, I spent a couple of minutes mopping other areas of the floor that looked dirty, including mopping up a few crumbs by the toaster. Those crumbs seemed to trigger a hunger pang and I decided to put some bread into the toaster so I could have toast with my coffee as I had my devotional time. While the bread was in the toaster, I turned on the television to catch a little more news. I became absorbed in what I was seeing and by the time I looked again at the clock, I really had to scramble to get my shower, get dressed, and get out the door.

"I grabbed my Bible as I picked up my briefcase, and decided on the way to work that I'd pray a little—but I first turned on the radio to see if there were any traffic problems I needed to know about, and by the time I got the traffic report and made a quick stop at the bakery to take donuts to the office, I realized that any attempts at prayer would not have my full concentration, so, I determined I'd spend some time reading my Bible and praying during the noon hour. A colleague asked me to lunch at 11:45 and I didn't feel I could refuse. I decided I'd have my devotional time as soon as I got home.

"Well, I couldn't get away from work until almost seven o'clock. On the way home I remembered I needed to pick up the dry cleaning and get a couple of items at the grocery store. I was later than usual getting home and the dog needed to be let out again and I was hungry. While dinner was in the microwave, I sorted quickly through my mail and heard the messages on my answering machine. As I ate dinner, I returned phone calls I needed to respond to and checked my home computer for e-mail. I spent a few minutes surfing the net. Then I put in a load of laundry, got my clothes ready for the next day, wrote out a check for a past-due bill that came in the mail, jotted a few quick reminders to myself about the day ahead, read the five memos I needed to read before an early morning meeting, and got the coffee pot set up.

"By now it was ten thirty and I was yawning. I crawled into bed and opened my Bible and read . . . at least I think I did. I awoke again at twelve-forty to take off my glasses, turn out the light, and say, 'Good night, Lord. I'll do better tomorrow. I promise.'"

Been there, done that?

How is our current pace of life contrary to the concept of abiding?

How can we do a better job of abiding in Christ Jesus?

Is abiding a concept only for individuals, or is it for families and churches?

S
Supplementary Scriptures to Consider

Jesus not only said to abide in His Word, but also in His love:

> [Jesus said,] "As the Father loved Me, I also have loved you; abide in My love. If you keep My commandments, you will abide in My love, just as I have kept My Father's commandments and abide in His love" (John 15:9–10).

• How important is it to abide in Jesus' commandments *and* His love? How does an awareness of Christ's love make it easier to obey His commands?

• In what ways is love a vital component as we keep God's commandments regarding the way we treat other people?

Through the prophet Jeremiah, the Lord asked this of His people:

> "Yet I planted you a noble vine, a seed of highest quality.
> How then have you turned before Me into the degenerate
> plant of an alien vine?" (Jeremiah 2:21)

Do you know a person who seemed to begin his life of faith in Christ Jesus as *a seed of highest quality*, only to degenerate into an *alien vine*? What happened? Can this same thing happen to any person? Why or why not? In what ways are we all subject to degenerating influences? What can we do to keep from becoming attached to an alien vine?

The psalmist linked abiding with trusting God and receiving His protection:

> He who dwells in the secret place of the Most High shall abide under the shadow of the Almighty. I will say of the LORD, "He is my refuge and my fortress; My God, in Him I will trust."
> "Because you have made the LORD, who is my refuge, even the Most High, your dwelling place, No evil shall befall you, Nor shall any plague come near your dwelling; For He shall give His angels charge over you, to keep you in all your ways" (Psalm 91:1–2, 9–11).

• In what ways does fear keep us from being fruitful?

• In what ways is our faithfulness linked to courage?

I
Introspection and Implications

1. Jesus said, "As the branch cannot bear fruit of itself, unless it abides in the vine, neither can you, unless you abide in Me" (John 15:4). Can a person truly produce anything good and lasting apart from God's help?

2. Is there a difference between *good* fruit and *godly* fruit?

3. How might abiding in Christ Jesus be an antidote for stress?

4. Jesus said, "If you abide in Me, and My words abide in you, you will ask what you desire, and it shall be done for you" (John 15:7). Have you found this to be true in your life? If you are truly abiding in the Lord, will *your* desires match *His* desires? If you truly are abiding in the Lord, will you ask anything contrary to what He desires to do?

5. What keeps you from being as fruitful as you'd like to be? What can you do to become more fruitful?

6. What keeps you from being as faithful as you'd like to be? What can you do to be more steadfast in your faith walk?

C
Communicating the Good News

When people evaluate your life, do they judge you more by your deeds or your words? In what ways are words *fruit*? In what ways might deeds be more potent than words as *fruit*?

The purpose of fruit is to nourish others. What more might you do—individually or as a small group or as a church—to nourish others?

Jesus said, "By this my Father is glorified, that you bear much fruit; so you will be My disciples" (John 15:8). What does this statement mean to you in your efforts to lead people to Christ and to make disciples?

LESSON #7

JESUS IS THE SACRIFICIAL LAMB FOR THE FORGIVENESS OF SIN

*Sacrifice: a freewill offering of something valuable
or important to gain something deemed
even more valuable or important*

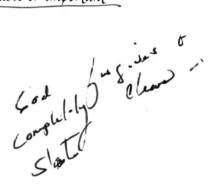

B
Bible Focus   *Forgets!! (?*

> The next day John saw Jesus coming toward him, and said,
> "Behold! The Lamb of God who takes away the sin of the
> world!" (John 1:29)
> Now early in the morning He came again into the temple,
> and all the people came to Him; and He sat down and taught
> them. Then the scribes and Pharisees brought to Him a
> woman caught in adultery. And when they had set her in the
> midst, they said to Him, "Teacher, this woman was caught in
> adultery, in the very act. Now Moses, in the law, commanded
> us that such should be stoned. But what do You say?" This
> they said, testing Him, that they might have something of
> which to accuse Him. But Jesus stooped down and wrote on
> the ground with His finger, as though He did not hear.
> So when they continued asking Him, He raised Himself up
> and said to them, "He who is without sin among you, let him
> throw a stone at her first." And again He stooped down and
> wrote on the ground. Then those who heard it, being convicted
> by their conscience, went out one by one, beginning with the
> oldest even to the last. And Jesus was left alone, and the woman
> standing in the midst. When Jesus had raised Himself up and
> saw no one but the woman, He said to her, "Woman, where are
> those accusers of yours? Has no one condemned you?"
> She said, "No one, Lord." And Jesus said to her, "Neither
> do I condemn you; go and sin no more" (John 8:1–11).

The Gospel of John places extremely high value on the truth that Jesus died so men and women might be forgiven of their sin and receive the gift of eternal life. John knew with certainty that to live and die in an unforgiven state was to reap the consequences of sin—eternal separation from God the Father. He knew with equal certainty that to be forgiven was to reap the rewards of everlasting life. John said Jesus did not come to condemn the world but rather, to die a sacrificial, atoning death so those who seek God's forgiveness might receive it.

At the outset of his Gospel account, John recorded the words of John the Baptist who said of Jesus, "Behold! The Lamb of God who takes away the sin of the world!" (John 1:29) John also recorded the words of John the Baptist spoken about Jesus *the next day*, Behold! the Lamb of God (John 1:29). Why was this title of *Lamb* so important?

A lamb was considered the supreme sacrificial animal to the Jews.

Through thousands of years, lambs had been sacrificed for the atonement of sin on the Day of Atonement. During Passover—the major springtime feast God established for an annual celebration—unblemished lambs were offered to the Lord in commemoration of God delivering the Israelites from Egyptian bondage. The night before the Israelites left Egypt, those who had the blood of a lamb on the doorposts and lintels of their home were spared the ravaging work of the death angel. (See Exodus 12.) The church readily saw Jesus as being the ultimate Passover Lamb. He was sacrificed so a person might be set free from the bondage of sin and, in turn, begin a journey to the Land of Promise in which all things blessed and abundant are found.

Throughout the Gospel of John, Jesus is portrayed as the Savior who provides atonement for sin and allows people to become reconciled fully to God the Father. Jesus is presented as the Savior who provides for the forgiveness of sin, ensures a life free of sin's bondage, and secures everlasting life for those who believe in Him. Jesus said to the Jews who were persecuting Him and seeking to kill him, "Most assuredly, I say to you, he who hears My word and believes in Him who sent Me has everlasting life, and shall not come into judgment, but has passed from death into life" (John 5:24).

One of the most profound stories of forgiveness in the Gospels is the account of Jesus forgiving a woman brought to Him for judgment. She had been caught *in the very act* of adultery by a group of scribes and Pharisees. The man involved in the adulterous affair had not been brought before Jesus—the purpose of the scribes and Pharisees was not to attain justice, but rather, to trick Jesus into contradicting the Law of Moses and thus, losing favor with the crowds in the temple.

In a few minutes, and using very few words, Jesus taught two critically important lessons about forgiveness.

First, forgiveness and love are inseparably linked from God's point of view.

Jesus stooped and wrote in the dust on the ground with His finger. *What He wrote was not important;* if it had been, John would have recorded it. The fact Jesus wrote in the *dust* and wrote with His *finger* are important.

The Jews knew when God met with Moses on Mount Sinai, He had given Moses *two tablets of the Testimony, tablets of stone, written with the finger of God* (Exodus 31:18). The Law, set in stone, was absolute and never to be violated. It spelled out punishments related to life and death.

The Jews also knew when God created man, He *formed man of the dust of the ground* (Genesis 2:7).

Here is Jesus, God in the flesh, writing with His finger into the dust of humanity's heart a new law of love. The law of stone was not being abolished; rather, a law of love was being added so mankind might *want* to keep the law and be *enabled* to keep the law, rather than fight against it or be oppressed by it.

Jesus, in His response to the woman's accusers, does not negate the Law of Moses. Rather, He says, "He who is without sin among you, let him throw a stone at her first" (John 8:7). The truth was, all her accusers had sinned, and were just as guilty and just as worthy of having the stones of Moses' tablets thrown at them. Hate compels us to accuse and condemn. Love compels us to forgive. Jesus shifted the issue from sin and hateful accusation resulting in death, to sin and loving forgiveness resulting in life.

Second, a person can be forgiven of sin and set free of sin's bondage.

Jesus said to the woman, "Go and sin no more" (John 8:11). He did not deny the fact she had sinned. Nor did He say her sin didn't matter. Nor did He say her sin didn't have consequences. Rather, Jesus said He did not condemn her and that she should go and sin no more.

Accusation and condemnation harden the heart—both of the accuser and the accused. Condemnation leads to further sin. The cycle is an endless downward spiral.

Jesus taught loving forgiveness that produces a real change of heart—in both the forgiver and the forgiven—and genuine freedom to pursue a new life. Forgiveness heals, restores, and renews. The cycle is an *upward* spiral.

The motivation for God's forgiveness is love. (See John 3:16.)

The result of God's forgiveness is life—renewed life now, heavenly life forever.

What motivates us to receive God's forgiveness? Our need for love and restoration to God.

What enables us to live a new life? Knowing we are not under condemnation, but that we have been set free from sin's bondage. Knowing we are loved. Knowing we will live with Christ Jesus forever.

A
Application for Today

When the Moravian missionaries first went to the Eskimos with the gospel, they could not find a word in their language for forgiveness. They compounded one. The word turned out to be: *Issumagijoujungnainermik.* The word literally means: *not being able to think about it anymore.*

People today often say, "Oh, I can forgive, but I'll never forget."

However, God forgets when He forgives. The Bible tells us God *remits* our sins—He removes them so completely that we stand before Him spotless and clean, as if we have never sinned. God does not keep a running account of our sins and good deeds. He looks at our relationship with His Son, Jesus Christ, and rewards us on the basis of what Jesus has done in us and through us, not on what we have done in our own strength.

When we forgive another person, we must no longer hold that person's sin against him. We must let it go and refuse to harbor its remembrance.

When we forgive ourselves, we must turn our own thoughts away from our past deeds and choose to let God heal our emotions from any guilt or shame we once felt.

Jesus did not die a sacrificial death on the cross to whitewash our sins, but to cleanse us so we were *whiter than snow*, or as *white as snow*. (See Psalm 51:7 and Isaiah 1:18.)

How difficult is it to forgive?

How difficult is it to forgive and forget?

What aspects of sin are we wise to remember—and why?

What aspects of sin are we wise to forget—and why?

S
Supplementary Scriptures to Consider

The apostle Paul reminded the Corinthians of Jesus' sacrificial death:
Christ, our Passover, was sacrificed for us (1 Corinthians 5:7).

• By definition, a sacrifice is a freewill offering of something valuable or important to gain something deemed even more valuable or important.

Jesus gave up His life—no one took it from Him. His life, of infinite importance, was made a sacrifice so God the Father might gain back His lost and sinful creation, mankind. What does it mean to know God sacrificed His only begotten Son, Jesus, so you might live in a loving, forgiven relationship with Him? How does it feel to know God thought you were of such significant value He sent His Son to die for you?

- In what ways do we as Christians *sacrifice* today as part of our worship?

  Fast

This psalm is attributed to King David after the prophet Nathan had confronted him about his sin. It is considered the great prayer of repentance in the Psalms:

> Have mercy upon me, O God,
> According to Your lovingkindness;
> According to the multitude of Your tender mercies.
> Blot out my transgressions.
> Wash me thoroughly from my iniquity,
> And cleanse me from my sin.
>   For I acknowledge my transgressions,
> And my sin is always before me.
> Against You, You only, have I sinned,
> And done this evil in Your sight—
> That You may be found just when You speak,
> And blameless when You judge.
>   Behold, I was brought forth in iniquity,
> And in my sin my mother conceived me.
> Behold, You desire truth in the inward parts,
> And in the hidden part You will make me to know wisdom.
>   Purge me with hyssop, and I shall be clean;
> Wash me, and I shall be whiter than snow.
> Make me hear joy and gladness,
> That the bones You have broken may rejoice.
> Hide Your face from my sins,
> And blot out all my iniquities.
>   Create in me a clean heart, O God,
> And renew a steadfast spirit within me.
> Do not cast me away from Your presence,
> And do not take Your Holy Spirit from me.
>   Restore to me the joy of Your salvation,

And uphold me by Your generous Spirit,
Then I will teach transgressors Your ways,
And sinners shall be converted to You.
   Deliver me from the guilt of bloodshed, O God,
The God of my salvation,
And my tongue shall sing aloud of Your righteousness.
O Lord, open my lips,
And my mouth shall show forth Your praise.
For You do not desire sacrifice, or else I would give it;
You do not delight in burnt offering.
The sacrifices of God are a broken spirit,
A broken and a contrite heart—
These, O God, You will not despise.
   Do good in Your good pleasure to Zion;
Build the walls of Jerusalem.
Then You shall be pleased with the sacrifices of righteousness,
With burnt offering and whole burnt offering;
Then they shall offer bulls on Your altar (Psalm 51).

- Are there particular phrases that stand out as you read through this psalm? If not, read through it again slowly and aloud. Reflect on any statements that seem especially pertinent to you or that bring questions to your mind.

purge me
Cleanse
Mercy

- What does this psalm say about sacrifice? How does an attitude of your heart relate to sacrifice? What are *sacrifices of righteousness*? (Psalm 51:19)

Set asides
Obidence

Jesus taught this to His disciples about sins (offenses) and forgiveness between human beings:

> Then He said to the disciples, "It is impossible that no offenses should come, but woe to him through whom they do come! It would be better for him if a millstone were hung around his neck, and he were thrown into the sea, than that he should offend one of these little ones. Take heed to yourselves. If your brother sins against you, rebuke him; and if he repents, forgive him. And if he sins against you seven times in a day, and seven times in a day returns to you, saying, 'I repent,' you shall forgive him" (Luke 17:1–4).

- Millstones were used for grinding corn; to have one tied around your neck and to be thrown into the sea meant certain drowning. *Little ones* are not only children, but new believers of any age. Why is it especially important that we not sin against the innocent or the new believer?

for they do not know better things. Correct

- How difficult is it at times to *rebuke* those who sin against you?

Very — get mad

- How can you tell if a person has truly repented? How do you display repentance for your sins?

  behavior ?

- What form of repentance does God seek from those He has forgiven?

  behavior –
  confession

Jesus taught this parable about forgiveness:

> Then Peter came to Him and said, "Lord, how often shall my brother sin against me, and I forgive him? Up to seven times?"
>
> Jesus said to him, "I do not say to you, up to seven times, but up to seventy times seven. Therefore the kingdom of heaven is like a certain king who wanted to settle accounts with his servants. And when he had begun to settle accounts, one was brought to him who owed him ten thousand talents. But as he was not able to pay, his master commanded that he be sold, with his wife and children and all that he had, and that payment be made. The servant therefore fell down before him, saying, 'Master, have patience with me, and I will pay you all.' Then the master of that servant was moved with compassion, released him, and forgave him the debt.
>
> "But that servant went out and found one of his fellow servants who owed him a hundred denarii; and he laid hands

on him and took him by the throat, saying, 'Pay me what you owe!' So his fellow servant fell down at his feet and begged him, saying, 'Have patience with me, and I will pay you all.' And he would not, but went and threw him into prison till he should pay the debt. So when his fellow servants saw what had been done, they were very grieved, and came and told their master all that had been done. Then his master, after he had called him, said to him, 'You wicked servant! I forgave you all that debt because you begged me. Should you not also have had compassion on your fellow servant just as I had pity on you?' And his master was angry, and delivered him to the torturers until he should pay all that was due to him.

"So My heavenly Father also will do to you if each of you, from his heart, does not forgive his brother his trespasses" (Matthew 18:21–35).

- Rabbinic tradition taught a repeated sin should be forgiven three times, but on the fourth, there was to be no forgiveness. Peter likely thought seven times was being overly generous. What about you? How difficult is it to forgive a repeat offender who continually sins against you?

- One of these servants owed a great deal—in today's money, possibly millions of dollars. The other owed very little. How difficult is it for us to forgive what we perceive to be a *great* sin? How easy is it for us to ignore our own sin and demand perfection from others?

• What does it mean to you to forgive *from your heart*? (Matthew 18:35)

Tough --
Complete

I
Introspection and Implications

1. Have you ever had someone die so that you might live? If so, how do you feel about that? If not, how do you think you would feel if that happened?

   No —

2. Do you believe Jesus' sacrificial atoning death was for *you*? Has God forgiven your sins, based on your faith in Jesus as the Son of God, who gave His life for you? If you haven't done so already, is today the day for you to believe and receive God's forgiveness?

   yes

3. In what ways do you struggle to forgive others as freely as God the Father has forgiven you?

Very hard

C
Communicating the Good News

Reflect on this statement: "There's nothing as awesome as knowing that God has made a way for us to live without guilt, without shame, and without a compulsion to sin." How might a person express the tremendous freedom we have in Christ Jesus to someone who does not know that freedom? What does freedom mean to a person who has never been free, and has no understanding of spiritual freedom?

Jesus taught about the Father's great desire to save the lost:

> [Jesus said,] "Take heed that you do not despise one of these little ones, for I say to you that in heaven their angels always see the face of My Father who is in heaven. For the Son of Man has come to save that which was lost.
>
> "What do you think? If a man has a hundred sheep, and one of them goes astray, does he not leave the ninety-nine and go to the mountains to seek the one that is straying? And if he should find it, assuredly, I say to you, he rejoices more over that sheep than over the ninety-nine that did not go astray. Even so it is not the will of your Father who is in heaven that one of these little ones should perish" (Matthew 18:10–14).

If it is not the *Father's* will that any should perish, what does this say about what *our* will should be?

The Same

If the purpose of Jesus' coming was to *save that which was lost* (Matthew 18:11), what does this say about what our life purpose should be?

Evangelise ___

NOTES TO LEADERS
OF SMALL GROUPS

As the leader of a small discussion group, think of yourself as a facilitator with three main roles:

- Get the discussion started

- Involve every person in the group

- Encourage an open, candid discussion that remains focused on the Bible

You certainly don't need to be the person with all the answers! In truth, much of your role is to ask questions, such as:

- What impacted you most in this lesson?

- What part of the lesson did you find troubling?

- What part of the lesson was encouraging or insightful?

- What part of the lesson would you like to explore further?

Express to the group at the outset of your study that your goal as a group is to gain new insights into God's Word—this is not the forum for defending a point of doctrine or a theological opinion. Stay focused on what God's Word says and means. The purpose of the study is also to share insights of how to apply God's Word to everyday life. *Every* person in the group can and should contribute—the collective wisdom that flows from Bible-focused discussion is often very rich and deep.

Seek to create an environment in which every member of the group feels free to ask questions of other members to gain greater understanding. Encourage group members to voice their appreciation to one another for new insights gained, and to be supportive of one another personally. Take the lead in doing this. Genuinely appreciate and value the contributions each person makes.

You may want to begin each study by having one or more members of the group read through the section provided under "Bible Focus." Ask the group specifically if it desires to discuss any of the questions under the "Application for Today" section, the "Supplemental Scriptures to Consider" section, the "Introspection and Implications" and "Communicating the Good News" section. You do not need to come to a definitive conclusion or consensus about any question asked in this study. Rather, encourage your group if it does not have a satisfactory Bible-based answer to a question that the group engage in further asking, seeking, and knocking strategies to discover the answers. Remember the words of Jesus: "Ask, and it will be given to you; seek, and you will find; knock, and it will be opened to you. For everyone who asks receives, and he who seeks finds, and to him who knocks it will be opened" (Matthew 7:7–8).

Finally, open and close your study with prayer. Ask the Holy Spirit, whom Jesus called the Spirit of Truth, to guide your discussion and to reveal what is of eternal benefit to you individually and as a group. As you close your time together, ask the Holy Spirit to seal to your remembrance what you have read and studied, and to show you ways in the upcoming days, weeks, and months how to apply what you have studied to your daily life and relationships.

General Themes for the Lessons

Each lesson in this study has one or more core themes. Continually pull the group back to these themes. You can do this by asking simple questions, such as, "How does that relate to _____?", "How does that help us better understand the concept of _____?", or "In what ways does that help us apply the principle of _____?"

A summary of general themes or concepts in each lesson follows:

Lesson #1
JESUS IS GOD'S WORD

The power of words to influence

The power of words to inflict pain

The power of words to encourage

The power of words to create

The importance of speaking words that promote life

Lesson #2
JESUS IS THE TRUE LIGHT

What Jesus revealed about God, about us, about how to relate to God, and about how to relate to others

Opening one's eyes to an understanding of what is true

The importance of speaking words that bring truth to light

Lesson #3
JESUS IS THE BREAD OF LIFE FROM HEAVEN

The basics of good spiritual nutrition

Instant versus delayed gratification

Our need for daily bread, including daily spiritual food

Lesson #4
JESUS IS THE GOOD SHEPHERD

Our responsibility to follow Jesus as our Shepherd every day

Our responsibility to serve those who follow us

Lesson #5
JESUS IS THE LIFE–GIVER

Resurrection

The importance of walking away from deadly sinful habits and being loosed to live fully in Christ

Jesus being the Way, Truth, and Life

Lesson #6
JESUS IS THE VINE

Abiding in Christ Jesus

　Abiding in His words

　Abiding in His love

Faithfulness

Fruitfulness

Lesson #7
JESUS IS THE SACRIFICIAL LAMB FOR THE FORGIVENESS OF SIN

Forgiveness

Sacrifice

Forgiving and Forgetting

Repentance

NOTES